Published by Hallmark Gift Books,
a division of Hallmark Cards, Inc.,
Kansas City, MO 64141
Visit us on the Web at Hallmark.com.

Editorial Director: Delia Berrigan
Editor: Jennifer Snuggs
Art Director: Jan Mastin
Designer: Rob Latimer
Production Designer: Dan Horton

ISBN: 978-1-59530-581-7
BOK1251

Printed and bound in China

85 Friends
Of Hallmark Say

thanks,
Mom

*Letters, Poems,
and Short Stories
of Gratitude*

TABLE OF CONTENTS

Thanks for Being . . .

THANKS FOR BEING

My

Teacher

Mom,

I didn't want to make you get up, so I have placed this letter next to your easy chair in hopes you will notice it. Now that you have, please note I wiped my shoes on the mat before I came in. So, put your feet up and enjoy, because you deserve it!

I want you to know that I always shut the door behind me; I have learned heating the outdoors is a waste of money. Friends and acquaintances would never guess I was born in a barn. I am not considered a slouch, I sit up straight, shoulders back, and I look people in the eyes when I speak. I no longer twirl my hair, bite my nails, or fidget! I eagerly try new foods without hesitation, because I realize there is a chance I might like it. I am a leader in my community, and if so and so jumps off a cliff, so be it! I will say I haven't melted yet—as sweet as you tell me I am, I know I am not made of sugar. I understand all parts of NO and that nobody died and left me boss. I realize that rules were not made to be broken, and that is only because I am older now. I don't cry over spilt milk, and when I am sorry, I say it like I mean it.

When I make my bed, I know I have to lay in it and have many times. I still go out "dressed like that"; something we will never see eye-to-eye on. I promise I didn't live to annoy you, but making you crazy at times was humorous. Yes, I know this will come back to me tenfold and has. If you have told me once, you have told me a thousand times that you love me. I know, Mom, that nobody loves me more.

With all you have done, all you have said, you have made a believer out of me. No need to explain yourself. You always wanted what was best for me and loved me no matter what.

A little birdie told me that it was time to say thank you, Mom. I now have kids of my own, and I understand. If wishes were horses, I would wish everyone had a mother like you! I am doing this for your own good!

Thank you, Mom,
Your loving daughter

Rebecca Farrell - Newark, DE

Advice from you met with rolling eyes,
  impatience and exaggerated sighs . . .
Disrespectful, but part of my growth,
  this disruptive wedge between us both . . .

But now I hear you loud and clear
  the things you told me year after year . . .
  I stop and grab a coat (in case),
  and your words begin to fall in place:

"Why buy the cow if the milk's for free?"
"You get more honey from a satisfied bee."
"Watch where you park, stranger danger is near!"
"The living, not dead, are the ones to fear."

Unsolicited advice was doled out in years
  from too much pops to too many beers . . .
  and I listened, I did, though not very well,
Somewhere, in the back of my mind, those words fell.

They piled up and now have compiled
  a list of things for my own stubborn child.
So it goes, between every mother, daughter, and son,
  a battle of words eventually won.
  By Mom.

Grace Fulljames - Henderson, NV

My mom, with her thick German accent, always gave us girls her motherly advice, using her sweet and funny analogies. My favorite was in the early 70s when I was in college and about to move away from home. She told me, "You know, Patty, I was 18 years old and a virgin the first time I got married."

I thought, "Uh, oh . . . here we go."

She continued with, "And that was not such a good idea. It's like going into a shoe store and buying a pair of shoes without trying them on first."

I just burst out in laughter. This was coming from my mom, who was always so strict! As we both laughed, she looked at me seriously and said, "Now, I'm not saying it's okay to go out and try on every shoe . . . you can window-shop, too."

I really miss my mom and all of her sweet, funny analogies.

Patty Cimlov-Zahares - San Jose, CA

Mama,

While I was growing up, I know I was a total heathen. I rolled my eyes back in my head, smarting off, and thought I knew everything. I want you to know I'm sorry for all that and to let you know I was paying attention when you were trying to teach me the things I would have to know as an adult.

I learned patience, because you sure had a lot of it while I was learning to cook! My suppers for you and Daddy consisted of 3 kinds of beans, 2 kinds of potatoes and burned chicken, raw on the inside. You ate it all, well almost all, because you knew eventually I would get better.

I learned about admiration, for I always admired you for going to work every single day, sick or not. I knew you wanted to be at home with us but couldn't afford it. I know your heart wasn't at your job. I learned what understanding means when you sat me down to ask me if my feelings would be hurt if I only received one gift for Christmas. We didn't have enough money for all the kids, and I was the oldest at home. Well, Mama, I was hurt, but it wasn't because of only getting one gift. It was because you were hurting because you had to ask me in the first place.

I learned that all bad actions have consequences, like when I kept going into the woods to swing on grapevines, climb trees, and you knew I would come home with weed poisoning. When I went to go pick up the jug of cow's milk, and I was driving too fast, so it spilled in the car. That smell never came out, so we had to sell it. You taught me about the love for a mama's child, when I ran across the street right in front of a car, and it hit me right into a mudhole with gravel in it. I was banged up but was okay. You cried long after I had stopped. You cradled me in your arms all the way to the hospital and back. I told you I was okay, but that just made you cry that much more.

That's when I knew you loved me to the moon and back, and nobody anywhere could love me like that, but my mama.

Thank You, Mama

Deana Scott - Quincy, IN

Dear Mom,

As I am now a grown woman and mother of two, I want you to know a few things I've learned:

1. You are not stupid, as my evil teen persona believed you to be.
2. You are not blind, as I always blamed you for being when I showed up wearing the latest ridiculous trends.
3. You are not deaf, as I believed you were, when I was begging for just ONE more hour past curfew.
4. You are not judgmental, as I labeled you for just trying to instill morals in me.
5. You ARE the reason I am the mother and woman I am today.

Thank you, Mother, for enduring, endearing, and loving unconditionally. Without you, I wouldn't be.

Jennifer Bloech - Wilmington, NC

You taught me how to tie my shoes
Before Velcro was created
You brought me to the movies
(But not the ones R-rated!)

You showed me how to make the
Best chocolate chip cookies around
And watched me dance to Neil Diamond tunes
Before iPods made a sound

You told me to "be wise" when I would
Go out on a date
And you put me on restrictions
When I would come home late

You dried my tears through breakups
And told me to have faith
Your strength inspired me to trust
It would be worth the wait

Your prayers kept me safe as I went my way
And found my grown-up life
You looked beautiful and so happy
The day I became a wife

You've been there for me since I was a girl
And you've been there for my kids, too
For all your love and faithfulness
I want to say, "thank you"

Jennifer Wooller - Holyoke, MA

Dear Mom,

You told me that I'd thank you someday for all the advice you've given me through the years. I have compiled a list of the most important things that you've taught me so I can properly thank you.

1. You're going to sit there until you eat all of your brussels sprouts and remember that there are starving children in Africa.
2. Do I look like a maid?
3. Bring plenty of clean underwear.
4. I have eyes in the back of my head.
5. Watch for deer and call me when you get there.
6. Cross your eyes again and your face will freeze like that.
7. Did you flush?
8. Go ask your father.
9. Over my dead body!
10. Put that down! You don't know where it's been.
11. Swear on the Bible, and if you lie, you're going to hell.
12. Make sure the stove is off.
13. I'll wash your mouth out with soap and water.
14. You'll understand when you get older.
15. One day, you'll thank me for this.

Well, Mom . . . I can honestly say that I haven't seen the eyes in the back of your head to this day, my face never really did freeze that way, and you did kind of look like a maid with that apron on. You also really should have bought a tastier bar of soap, because when I bit that sucker in half, I was on the toilet for several days, and I DID flush! I am still hoping that I don't go to hell for lying on the Bible or that I won't actually have to step over your dead body someday. Oh, and every time you told me to ask Dad . . . he said yes! Because of you, I will always have plenty of clean underwear, turn the stove off, and watch out for deer on the road.

So, thank you, Mom, for all of your wonderful advice and instilling the fear of God into me. You will be happy to know that I just started using the very same tactics on my children. Each night when I say my prayers, I pray to God that the kids do not call the cops on me. But most importantly, I also thank God for such a wonderful mom who always knew that I'd understand someday when I got older.

Sincerely,

Your loving daughter

Rita Vetsch - Monticello, MN

Just an hour before dinner
I started my attack
I crept into the kitchen
"You put that cookie back!"

Mom yelled from another room
I know she couldn't see
Only way she could have known
She must have ESP

I smacked my little brother
He didn't shed a tear
Now I'm sitting in timeout
How did she even hear?

I swear Mom's an alien
With eyes behind her head
Otherwise, she'd never know
I had climbed out of bed

Any time a dirty word
Got whispered under breath
She would be there with the soap
And a glare harsh as death

My mother can't be human
She's way too smart to be
I wish her intelligence
Would just rub off on me

So someday, when I have kids
I'll know just what to do
And my children will wonder
If I'm alien, too

For Mom, for everything

Ginny Tank - Belvidere, IL

Dear Mom,

You said a lot of things to me over the years. Some of them seemed so silly to me that they caused my eyes to roll back in my head (though they didn't stay that way).

You said, "You will never regret taking more piano lessons." I took piano lessons for seven years. I quit when I was fifteen, against your advice. You were right. It wouldn't have killed me to take another year or two, and I'd be glad for them now.

You said, "You can always add salt, but you can't take it out." You've passed on much cooking advice, but this one hit home the time I misread a recipe that included ¼ teaspoon of salt and added ¼ cup. My husband scooped a large amount of the resulting dip onto a chip and mildly commented, "It's just a little briny." You were right. I should have added the salt later.

You said, "What you kids do today is not dancing. When I was a kid, dancing meant that the girl linked her hands around the fellow's neck while the fellow linked his hands around the girl's middle. Then, we would sway or step side-to-side in time to the music." Last year, Matt and I took dancing lessons. Now we are able to fox trot, waltz, rumba, cha-cha, and swing. Again, you were right. We might have had rhythm, but dancing is a whole other wonderful thing.

You said, "You'll understand when you have one of your own." I vowed never to say, "Because I told you so." But the truth is, sometimes there's no explanation that the child will understand, especially if the child is a teenager. Then, you have a child of your own and you say, "Oh, right, I get it now." The lightbulb glows over your head.

So, Mom, you were right. I am sorry I didn't get it then, but I get it now. Thank you.

Love,
Susie

Sue Curtis - Troy, OH

Warmed up bottles, printed diapers,
Soapy washcloths, sweet shampoo.
Baby powder, combing hair knots, patting curls down,
"Where's your shoe?"

Little dresses, starched and pretty,
Lacy socks and undies, too.
Dropped the puppy, he was wriggly,
"What am I to do with you?"

Shared red ice pops, cones with jimmies,
Cotton candy colored blue.
"Don't fill up on junk 'fore dinner,"
"Don't get up before we're through."

Tummy achin', "See, I warned you," yes, she did,
(and often, too).
Warm compresses, "Just an earache,"
Skinned knees-sores-cuts, "Oh, boohoo!"

Bandaged covered, (first kissed better)
"Take this stuff, it's good for you."
Oil, (it tastes like cod's old livers) little aspirins,
"Got the flu."

On and on for years we wandered,
Danced the Mom Dance, me and you.
Always something, tears we squandered,
Ups and downs (p.m. curfew).

Now here I am. Grown up. Without you.
Not doing what I'm 'sposed to do:
Warm up bottles, change cute diapers,
Soapy washcloths, sweet shampoo.

You did your best, there's no denying,
No one's even faulting you.
(You should have got an "A" for trying)
Come on, chin up, no "boohoo."

But I can never dance the Mom Dance,
Like the dance I danced with you.
You did your best, there's no denying,
I love you, Mom, merci beaucoup.

Jacquie Roland - Saugerties, NY

I realized I was out of luck
that fateful day that I said *%$#.
Mom stormed in with a bar of soap,
her patience at the end of its rope.

"That's not what I said," I tearfully cried!
She looked at me and knew that I lied.
I begged and I pleaded, "but I said 'duck stew!'"
She knew quite well that I'd said, "*%$# you."

She wrestled me down, nostrils a flarin',
(I was just glad it wasn't my butt that was barin'.)
Soap in my mouth? You think not so bad?
It was covered in hair and it made my mouth sad.

Twenty years later, when I hear someone swear,
I still taste armpit and little pit hairs.
I break out in hives at that four-letter word—
The trauma! The horror! (Yeah, I was a turd.)

So thanks Mom, for setting me straight right away.
My mouth surely got me in trouble that day . . .
But I grew up all right, my language quite clean!
You wield that soap like no one I've seen.

Bonnie Weise - Muskegon, MI

THANKS FOR BEING

My
Forgiver

Dear Mom,

It was me who broke the lamp, not the dog. I just needed to clear my conscience, because I want to be sure you love me forever. I know you value honesty; you've always inculcated that in me.

Love, your son Lorenzo

P.S. I know you also value timeliness. Although it took 17 years for this letter, I think I am improving. Perhaps keep an eye out for more letters . . .

Lorenzo Alviso - Rohnert Park, CA

When you walked into a flour-and-egg covered kitchen, and I was holding up a plate of blueberry pancakes for you for Mother's Day, you smiled and said it was the sweetest present you had ever had.

When you walked into my bedroom, and there were bits of colored paper and glue on the carpet, and I was holding up a heart-shaped Valentine's Day card with your only baby pictures pasted to the cover, you smiled and said it was the cutest present you had ever had.

When you walked into your bedroom, and I was holding up a fistful of tulips and marigolds picked from your carefully tended garden for your birthday, you said it was the most colorful present you had ever had.

And when you walked into the living room, and I had taken your jewelry and strung them together as Christmas ornaments, you said it was the prettiest present you had ever had.

But really, Mom, you are the perfect present, the best present a daughter could ever have.

Jaz Azari - Arlington, VA

Remember the day I turned the terrible twos into an art form? I'm sorry.

In a split second, I went from being "Shirley What's-Her-Name" to "Franken-Baby." Everyone loves a sweet baby. But no one loves a shrieking, screaming, crying, kicking, flailing, red-faced, totally out-of-control brat. Not even her mother. Her very young mother.

The day I fell in love with the pricey toy pony in front of the hardware store was EPIC. He had spots, brown glass eyes with lashes out to here, blond mane and tail, and, be still my heart, a real leather saddle—on bright red wheels. "HORSIE!" (I can still smell the fur.)

"Put her on it, let her ride," the storekeeper foolishly said. "It's OK." You knew better, didn't you, Mom?

He put me on . . . my heart swelled . . . I was on my horsie for a LONG time . . . long enough to draw that crowd. Way too long.

There comes a time when a mother, especially a young, inexperienced one, sees her life flash in front of her eyes. You knew you had to take me off. (It was that or just leave me there and move to Kansas.) It took guts. But you did it, didn't you. Even while the crowd was losing the love, was tut-tutting your inexperience, and I was shrieking my lungs out. (Can you say, "Hell on Wheels" . . . red ones?) It had to be done. You stepped up, did what you must. I was your responsibility. You took it. (Not gracefully, mind you, there was still that flailing thing to contend with.)

Was that the last time I embarrassed you? The only time I "showed myself"? I wish. Remember the dentist? (You called me "Jacqueline" for a long time after that.) After all these years, after all we've been through, what I want to say is, "Mom, I'm so sorry that I kicked the dentist and bit his nurse. I'm so sorry I peed on the horsie." You didn't really try to revoke my birth certificate that time . . . did you?

Thanks, Mom.

Jacquie Roland - Saugerties, NY

It was Friday on the last weekend of summer vacation 1969. I wanted a new pair of bell-bottom jeans for the first day of school. My old jeans were faded but still in good shape. Then it HIT ME. I could dye my old jeans with fabric dye, and they would LOOK new! I had enough money for a box of dye, so I purchased the navy blue dye and raced back home to turn my old jeans into a NEW pair of jeans!

I had the kitchen to myself all day. I found Mom's huge blue enamel roaster. It fit on both burners of the stove, and soon the dye was ready, and my jeans were transformed into bright navy blue denim! I scrubbed the pan, put it back, and cleaned up the kitchen. My jeans were ready for the first day back to school!

That Sunday, Mom had invited friends to Sunday dinner. Mom was THE greatest cook! As I helped her get the meal ready for the table, she opened the oven door to take a last-minute peek at the entrée she had prepared. I spotted the big, blue enameled roaster, and my heart LEAPED into my throat when she took the cover off and revealed a roaster full of bright NAVY BLUE Swiss steak!

We both stood frozen, staring at the contents as she asked me, "What could have caused this to happen?"

I stammered, "Maybe the USDA ink stamp on the meat was too strong!"

She looked at me long and hard. Then, she handed the roaster and her big quilted oven mitts to me and told me to go dump it in the field. (How could I have known that the dye would leach back out of the pan when the heat from the oven opened up the pores of the metal?) BUSTED.

I learned several things that day:

1. Without panicking, a full dinner can be created in just 20 minutes with what is in the cupboard and fridge.
2. The only person you fool when you fib is yourself.
3. A ruined dinner is equal in value to 6 babysitting jobs.
4. You can make something out of nothing. Just put a smile on your face and NEVER GIVE UP.

It was a hard lesson learned, but thank you, Mom, for everything you taught me that day!

Sandra Groth - Dorchester, WI

Dinnertime with four children is not the quiet and refined family time you see in old movies and TV shows. In our house, it was a cacophony of noise and a poorly choreographed ballet of arms and mouths in motion.

Mom tried valiantly to get us to use good manners. "Talk one at a time." "Ask someone to pass you food–don't reach." "Use your napkin, not your sleeve." Inevitably, disaster befell one of us. It wasn't unusual for a glass of milk to get knocked over, resulting in even more chaos as everyone jumped to throw napkins at the stream of milk before it cascaded over the edge of the table.

One night, Mom had had enough and declared, "The next one who spills will get spanked and sent to bed without dinner!"

We all sat silently looking down at our plates, each of us afraid to move for fear of spilling something. Suddenly, there was a crash, and what looked to be a tidal wave of milk was rolling across the table. Our eyes wide, we all looked around to see who had spilled. Lo and behold, it was MOM!

Mom got out of her chair to clean up the mess and then proceeded to spank herself saying, "Helen, I told you to be more careful. Now go to your room!"

We couldn't help ourselves. The giggles began and eventually burst into full-blown laughter. Dinner resumed in its usual lively state. We teased Mom for years about spilling and having to spank herself.

When we were grown, Mom finally confessed that she had spilled her milk on purpose. She said she felt bad that she had thrown down that ultimatum. We all looked scared and she realized that our time around the family dinner table should be fun. She also realized we would eventually outgrow our clumsy phases and ultimately move out. Having a quiet, spill-free dinner was not worth losing family time together.

Thanks, Mom, for teaching us that it really isn't useful to cry over spilled milk and for loving us enough to "take one for the team."

Donna Anderson - Frisco, TX

To anyone aside from my mom and myself, the following haiku wouldn't really make much sense, so allow me to explain. It was English class during my sophomore year of high school. We were entering "Poetry Week," and to celebrate, every day, a few selected people had to share either a published poem or an original work with the rest of the class.

I, being disorganized and forgetful, didn't remember that I had to share a poem that day. I didn't want to disappoint my class or make my teacher unhappy by telling her I had forgotten, so I recited a haiku I frantically made up on the spot. I entitled it "Meow":

I see elephants
Watermelons make good pets
Refrigerator

My classmates and teacher got a kick out of my pathetic attempt to be poetic, but I still got full credit for the assignment.

On the car ride home after school that day, I shared my experience with my mom, who couldn't contain her laughter at the thought of it. Of course, she was dying to know the haiku I had presented, but I refused to tell her, partially out of spite and a little bit of embarrassment. She has asked me to tell her as a birthday or Christmas gift, but I have continued to stand my ground and not tell her.

Mother's Day is coming up in a matter of weeks, and I have already purchased a gift for her, but she has been sending me obvious hints that she wants a framed copy of my haiku. Instead, why not share it with her and all moms during the season of Mother's Day to say "thank you for all you've done"?

Throughout my life, my mother has put up with my miscellaneous shenanigans, phases of rebellion, and silly acts of spite (like the "Meow" poem).

As I exit my teenage years and continue to mature, I know my mom and I will still have our differences. However, finally giving her the "Meow" poem is my way of thanking her for always being there for me, through both fun times and more serious troubles. Here you go, Mom.

Love,
Andrea

Andrea Semilia - Doylestown, OH

Muddy feet, sticky juice,
the floor's a mess, the gerbil's loose.

Whose fingerprints are on the wall?
They're not my prints; they're much too small.

Whose clothes are on the bathroom floor?
Who spilled shampoo? Who locked this door?

Mom will clean it. I am sure.
She's always there when we need her.

Who put a toothbrush down the drain?
Who colored on the windowpane?

Who ate the lubricating oil?
Who left the milk out? It will spoil.

Who hung up on the IRS?
Who made this great big awful mess?

Mom will fix it. I am sure.
She's always there when we need her.

Who glued the light switch? It won't budge.
Who sprayed the paint? Who ate the fudge?

You say your homework's due on Monday?
That's tomorrow. This is Sunday.

Science projects take some time
and now it's almost half past nine.

Mom will help me. I am sure.
She's always there when we need her.

Who put the cookies in our cart?
They're not healthy for your heart.

And who put donuts—look there's chips!
And fifteen lip balms for your lips!

I'll purchase one for you today.
Please don't knock down the store display.

Mom will buy it. I am sure.
She's always there when we need her.

Who's bleeding now? What did you do?
Glass isn't meant to be run through.

Who set that fire? Put it out.
I hope the smoke will soon clear out.

Your figurines have missing heads.
Have you looked underneath your beds?

Your rooms look like they've seen a war.
I cannot even see the floor.

Thank you, Mom, for being there.
Thank you for your constant care.

Though your work is never through,
remember that we love you, too!

Melinda Pritzel - Olathe, KS

THANKS FOR BEING

My Example

Dear Mom,

You have blessed me with a lifetime of precious knowledge. Because of you, I can make the world's best homemade fudge. You taught me the value of honesty, integrity, and frugality. Over the years, you have given me golden advice, a shoulder to cry on, and a friend to laugh with. I am the next generation couponer and bargain shopper. You taught me the value of a dollar and that confidence comes from earning it on my own.

Remember the trifold chaise hammock? I laugh every time I think back to that hot July afternoon. You always dreamed of lounging in your very own hammock, but money was tight. Priorities prevented such a purchase, but the dream didn't die. Just because you couldn't afford a hammock didn't mean you couldn't fashion one out of materials you already had lying around. Right, MacGyver?

So, you got some rope and that plastic trifold chaise. You set up shop between the two big trees in the backyard. After thirty minutes and a few minor tweaks, you were ready to relax in your new hammock. Without trepidation, you hopped on only to have the rope break. Somehow, your purple romper got twisted in the rope, and you found yourself in quite a predicament.

The "hammock story" isn't just an amusing tale. Whenever you wanted something, it didn't matter how many obstacles stood in the way, you went after it. You taught me to be just as tenacious in all my endeavors, and it has paid off! I even have a few amusing stories of my own to prove it. What I am trying to say is thanks, Mom, for all that you have done for me.

Love,
Jenn

Jennifer Harris - Hodgenville, KY

Thank you, Mom . . .
For helping me put on my flowered dress
For twirling my hair into a beautiful bun
For taking countless photographs
When I made my kindergarten debut, there you were
Smiling up at me from the audience
I could feel your pride from where I stood

Thank you, Mom . . .
For buying my black skirt and white top
For renting my violin
For listening to me practice
When I played in any concert, there you were
Smiling up at me from the audience
I could feel your pride from where I stood

Thank you, Mom . . .
For picking me up from rehearsal
For running lines with me
For taking me to the thrift store for costumes
When I acted in any play, there you were
Smiling up at me from the audience
I could feel your pride from where I stood

Thank you, Mom . . .
For taking a bus to Boston
For helping me pick out a dress
For wishing me good luck
When I stood up at that podium, there you were
Smiling up at me from the audience
I could feel your pride from where I stood

Thank you, Mom . . .
For proving that hard work pays off
For showing me that it is never too late
For giving me a role model
When you spoke at your graduation, there I was
Smiling up at you from the audience
I hope you could feel my pride from where you stood

Hannah Faiguenbaum - Huntington, NY

Mom,

It's been about 33 years, but I want to thank you for all the things you sacrificed for us.

I was about thirteen years old, and I was sitting on your bed talking to you. You had your underwear on, and you were putting on your pants. I noticed you had holes in your underwear, and I thought to myself, 'Why doesn't she go buy some new underwear,' and I think I even made a comment. You did not reply; all you did was smile.

Years later, I was getting dressed, and my son knocked on the door to thank me for his new boxer shorts and new jeans I had got him. I told him I did that because I love him. I continued to put my underwear on and my finger went right though my underwear. I just started to laugh because I finally realized why you had the holes in your underwear; it was because you loved us so much, you did without.

Thank you for being such a great mom.

Love you, your daughter,
Lisa

Lisa Mays - Franklin, VA

Mom,

I remember our trips "down south," and one in particular. We had traveled over 10 hours to get to great-grandmother's home, and without warning, our car slipped into a ditch. Night had set in and it was pitch black on that country road! As kids, we were so afraid. But not you, Mom! You immediately went into action.

You got us all out of the car. Then you had each one of us line up behind you with the oldest holding onto your waist and each one of us holding on to the one in front of us the same way. Out of nowhere, you found a stick and began to beat the ground in front of us as we marched single file towards the house! (Later, you told us you beat the ground to keep the snakes away!) Before any one of us could whimper or cry, we saw a kerosene lamp swinging back and forth and heard our great-grandmother's voice calling out to you. You followed her voice to the house . . . we were safe!

Mom, your lead is one we have all followed all our lives! Following your lead keeps us on the right path, keeps dangers at bay, and assures we will arrive at our destination safe and unharmed! You are truly our light and blessing, and I just wanted to let you know just how much you are loved and honored! I love you so much, Mom.

Your daughter,
Pat

Patricia Allen - Florissant, MO

It was a cold, snowy Christmas night, and we gathered around the dining room table to have a traditional Italian dinner. A Christmas tree twinkled in the front window of the adjoining room.

As we enjoyed dinner, the front door suddenly opened, and in walked a man. He was dressed in a dark raincoat with a hood. He pulled back the hood to reveal a young face. He was gloveless so his hands were reddened from the cold, and his shoes were snow-soaked. We had no idea who he was, so my son-in-law rose from his chair and cautiously moved towards him. But Mom held her hand up to stop him.

The boy walked up to Mom and said, "I'm hungry," and sat down next to her. Mom talked to him softly and asked what he wanted to eat. He pointed to the food and said, "All of it." Then he folded his hands and waited to be served. We sat in shock as Mom filled a plate for our unexpected guest. She set it before him, and he immediately ate his plate clean.

At this point, we realized that this young man was very special and might be a missing person. My sister quietly went into the other room and called the police. They confirmed that a mentally disabled man was missing and his mother was frantic to find him.

By the time the police and his distraught mother arrived, the young man had eaten two plates of food and was just about to have dessert. He was glad to see his mother but turned to Mom, gave her a hug and kiss on the cheek, and timidly said, "Thank you, I still want the cake."

His mother explained that he left without her knowledge and was walking to his dad's house fifty miles away. When she asked her son why he came to this house, pointing to Mom he replied, "I saw her in the window. She looked nice and I was hungry." Simple answer and so true. Mom didn't freak out but responded with kindness and caring. She taught us by example how to be the same, and we thank her for being such a wonderful mother.

Dolores Comparri - Richland, NJ

Dear Mom,

My divorce became final today, and because you were my support and inspiration, giving me the courage to leave that abusive relationship, I wanted to do something to show my gratitude. So, I got a tattoo.

Now, before you scream, "You did what?!" give me a chance to explain. I didn't get some nonsensical gibberish; this one has special meaning.

I know you rank tattoos right up there with bones through the nose or piercing of private parts, but you might actually like this one.

Remember when you divorced Dad? You didn't have the support of your family or friends because they didn't believe in divorce and it was frowned upon. You were scared, alone, with young kids to provide for, but you did it. I watched you go from insecure and meek to strong and independent—a woman reborn—a phoenix rising from the ashes.

That's what I got, Mom, a phoenix in honor of you.

No, a thank-you card would not have been enough. This way, I am reminded every day of your strength and what you accomplished and that I can do the same.

Maybe you think it's a bit much, but it's also a little bit for me as I begin my new life. You would probably have preferred flowers, so I ordered those, too; they'll arrive tomorrow.

Love,
"Li'l Phoenix"

Ginny Tank - Belvidere, IL

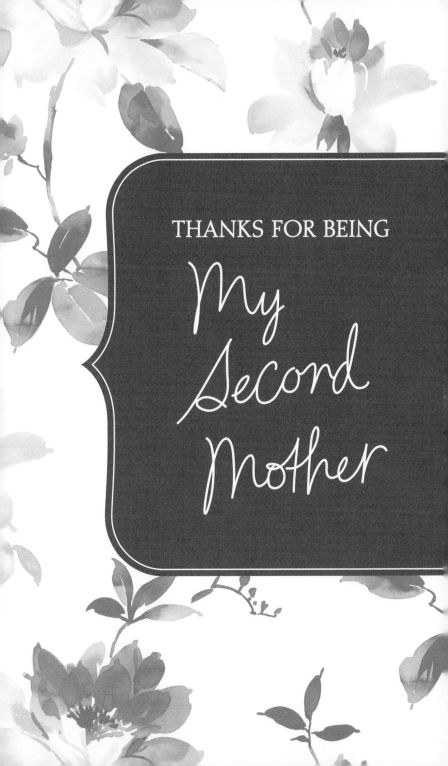

THANKS FOR BEING

My Second Mother

Pat,

To say you loved me like a mother would be something I can't really say. You loved me beyond the love my own mother showed me.

When I had my worst moments with illness or finances, you were the one who was there. You always had good advice for me and never judged me or turned your back on me.

You were the perfect example of what it is to be a mother.

Nothing I did would ever cost me your love. Every accomplishment was shouted to the mountaintops. You showed me how to be a good parent.

You also gave me the most precious gift of my life: your daughter, my wife. From you, she has learned to be just as accepting and loving. I am so fortunate to have the love and acceptance of both of you. And now I see that continued for a third generation as our daughter mothers her son.

Thank you for three generations of unconditional love and acceptance.

Larry Katz - Havertown, PA

Dear Grace,

Thank you for being a "mom" to us after we lost both of our mothers. You have been our next-door neighbor for over 40 years and have always been there for us!

You have watched us start out as newlyweds, been there to welcome all four of our daughters when each one was born. You gave us vegetables from your garden, cooked for us, and even babysat when we needed your help. You included us in your life events, and we felt like part of your family when there were birthdays and picnics. When you made it to your 90s, we enjoyed helping to care for you when you were ill or injured. Spending time with you was always fun, especially when we played Skip-Bo or Scrabble or you shared stories of your life from your earliest years.

Thank you for always caring about us. Thank you for calling us your kids. You are a very special mother who is loved not only by her own children and grandchildren but also by our whole family and also many other people in our neighborhood. We ask God to bless you in your new home where you moved last year to be closer to your son. We miss seeing you every day, but we are so thankful that you are being cared for and loved.

Rondy & Annette

Annette LaMore - Manteno, IL

I was at my future in-laws house during my birthday just a month after my fiancé had proposed. I opened a birthday gift from his parents and it was a beautiful silver locket with a "D," my first initial, engraved on top. As I took out the lovely necklace and put it on, his mom handed me another box. She said, "Here is a special gift I'm giving you a few months early."

Inside was another larger locket with three letters engraved on it. I looked closely, and I saw it read, "D.P.C.," the initials I would have once my fiancée and I were married. I started to tear up and glanced at my future mom-in-law who was teary-eyed, too. She hugged me and said, "I'm giving this to you now because I'm so happy you are going to be my daughter. I just couldn't wait— welcome to the family!"

Thank you, Hunny, for making me feel so welcomed and loved and for treating me like your own daughter. You're not just my mother-in-law, you're my mother-in-love, and I love you!

Devanee Chapman - Boerne, TX

Dear Best Friend's Mom,

You don't know what you did for me when you included me in your family functions. I would not have known a true family dynamic without your love and concern for me. Even though you did not have all the facts, you knew a few. I did not live with my parents. I lived with my grandparents. I was afraid to be home with my grandfather by myself. Anytime I asked, you were willing to let me go and spend the night or the weekend with your family.

When I ran away from home at 15, I know you prayed for my safety. Even when Karla and I messed up, you continued to love me like I was part of your family. Even now 40+ years later, you remember my birthday and include me in your family, and for that I want to say thank you . . . and I will always love you and your family like my own. Thanks for loving me enough to care.

Your other daughter,
Sue Jones

Sue Jones - Buffalo, IA

Dear Mom,

I've been thinking about those wonderful talks we used to have when I'd get home from a date. Back then, I took those talks for granted, but I now realize just how special they were.

As soon as I'd walk in the door, you'd call out from your bedroom, "Honey, did you have a good time?" I'd go in, sit on your bed, and tell you all about my night . . . okay, maybe I'd leave out just a few details!

Usually, I'd describe some silly thing that happened, and we'd laugh until we cried while Dad grunted, hinting he wanted to go back to sleep. We secretly thought he enjoyed listening to us, but we'd never have gotten him to admit it.

You never once fell asleep before I walked in the door. I'd like to think it was because of my amusing stories, but it's more likely that you wanted to be sure that I made it home safely.

Mom, the years have passed quickly. We've both had busy lives, but our relationship has continued to be as loving and strong as ever. You've been the one person who has always been there for me, and I thank you for that.

When your health declined a few years ago, our roles reversed. Now I have taken on the role as your caregiver. I love being able to care for you the way you did for me. I think I've learned well from the example you set, and I hope I'm making you proud.

We've come full circle, but there is no denying I still need my mom. After we get you settled into bed tonight, I'll sit down next to you, and we'll chat about something silly that happened during the day. I hope we laugh until we cry.

I love you,
Me

Connie Pullen - Eagle Creek, OR

Dear Margie,

Have I told you lately that I love you? You're Sam's momma but also my own. The kind of momma who believes it means something to be a family. And it means everything.

You're the momma who doesn't like to come inside when there's still plenty of sunshine to share. And the momma who knows the healing power of a gigantic grin, thoughtful word, or corny joke.

You're the momma who always leaves room at the table for one more. And the one who could live without socks but not the hugs, kisses, and voices of her more-precious-than-gold grandchildren.

You're the momma who finds it impossible to not tell it like it is. And you're the momma who loves talking to chickens almost as much as listening to the sound of rain.

You're a fisherwoman, fierce Scrabble competitor, and good friend. It means something to be a part of our family. And it means everything. You make it so.

You're the momma I'd most like to be. But I probably don't have to tell you all this, because you already know. You're that kind of momma.

Your eternally grateful daughter-in-law,
Leslie

Leslie McCrary - San Antonio, TX

THANKS FOR BEING

My
Clown

On a day long ago, you ran down the hall
In your support pantyhose, and I could see all.

You covered your bum, but it was too late,
I saw it all, the vision too great.

My retinas were burned and my corneas scorched,
I ran out of the house and sat on the porch.

And as I asked God why you're such a nut,
I couldn't stop thinking of your unibutt.

I shook my head, but there it remained
Like shards of glass picking my brain.

But now I'm older, and as I face woes,
I think of you running in those awful hose.

And suddenly, my day's bright and sunny,
So thanks for being you, Mom. Thanks for being funny.

Diane Reyerson-Warren - Canton, GA

My mother had a great sense of humor . . . not always on purpose. Like the time she told me I had a spider web in my hair. Of course, I screamed and shook my hair. I hate spiders . . . or any bugs for that matter!

"Is it gone???!!!!," I asked.

She looked straight at me and said, "No, you still have a spider web in your hair."

I ran to look in the mirror. I didn't see any spider webs, but I did happen to notice a pesky cowlick . . . one clump of hair sticking straight up that always seemed to plague me.

"Mom, I don't have any spider webs in my hair, just a cowlick."

She thought for a moment and smiled. "Oh, cowlick, I couldn't think of the word. I thought it was a spider web."

I like to think I inherited my mom's sense of humor. My children think I did. I think they get theirs from their grandmother!

Thanks, Momma. We did have lots of laughs together!

Jo Ann Aragona - Tannersville, PA

THANKS FOR BEING

My
Favorite
Recipe

Dear Mom,

Thanks for teaching me
important kitchen lessons.
Lessons like:
      cookies do not
      need to be baked
      to be enjoyed.

Love, Your Dough Girl

Jenny Fenlason - Minneapolis, MN

Dear Mom,

As I sit here thumbing through the many recipes you have saved throughout your life and through my childhood, I can't help but smile. The small wooden recipe box is chipped and faded. The index cards and magazine and newspaper clippings are discolored and yellowed and speckled with stains of what could have been egg or milk splattered when you were mixing up your creations. Your handwritten recipes dotted with your own little notations, "Add a teeny bit of sugar" or "Don't go crazy with too much salt," make me remember what a fun-spirited person you were.

I remember you making almost every single recipe in that tiny box of memories. Your appreciation of cooking and baking filled the air in our tiny apartment with warmth and love. You have passed that love down to me. As I make many of your recipes for my family and as the wondrous smells drift through my home, it brings me back in time to a time of warmth and love that makes me feel close to you. Mom, thank you for giving me the love of cooking and helping me make wonderful memories for my children. Tonight, I think I'll make your Chicken Cacciatore, and for dessert, your famous butter cookies!

Love,
Dorann

Dorann Weber - Brown Mills, NJ

I'm not very good in the kitchen you see,
But wait just a moment and listen to me.
It sounds really weird, but here's what she'd be,
If my mom was reduced to a mere recipe.

Take 2 C flour and add that to start —
A vital ingredient, just like a heart.
It taints all it touches and acts like a glue,
An innermost strength that holds all things true.

A tsp of baking soda, the next thing to add,
And if it's messed up, the food will taste bad.
It functions like feelings, effects have so showed —
Too little is bland and excess can explode.

A pinch of salt is then thrown in the mix
To enhance other flavors and give them their kicks.
Its measure is fitting, since sarcasm, too,
Can feel like a pinch when thrown right at you.

In a separate bowl, 2 sugars you add,
¾ C each, to sweeten a tad.
Its flavor and flair, a spirit of sorts;
A soft cookie inside it gives and supports.

2 sticks of butter you beat into this,
And since it's like patience, you shouldn't dismiss.
At times it is cold, and mixing is tough
If it isn't warmed up and softened enough.

1 tsp vanilla, though small, don't ignore;
Because it's my favorite, I always add more.
And just like my mother, this flavorful treat
Is humbly blended, though nothing but sweet.

Once that is well mixed, 2 eggs get beat in,
And just like a mind, they work from within.
They add shelf life and structure and richness and taste;
While not vital to use, without, it's a waste.

Now slowly mix both bowls together as one,
But don't get excited, it's still not quite done.
2 C choc chips—toss in and have fun!
A combo that's better? I swear there is none.

At temp 3-7-5, in 9 mins, when brown,
You'll want to have loved ones to share with around.
These cookies are great—quite frankly, da bomb,
Which is why they remind me so much of my mom.

She's sweet and she's loving, and strong, always there,
She reminds me "forever" is how long she'll care.
Her spirit is giving and kind like no other,
For all this and more, I say "Thank you, my mother."

Katelyn Stenger - Stow, OH

My mother doesn't use recipes. While she is an excellent cook, her dishes never turn out the same way twice. Learning the culinary arts from her requires close shadowing and careful observation. There have been countless times over the years when I've called to ask what to add to a certain dish, and her answer would be something like, "Oh, you know, maybe a dab of milk." What does that mean?

Homemade cookies were a regular afterschool ritual as we were growing up. I remember spooning the dough onto the cookie sheets as I talked about my day. The sheets were marked and blackened on the edges by years of use, and I loved them. We baked together so often that I became a capable cookie-maker at a very young age.

When I moved into my very first apartment as a young woman, my mom brought over a box full of essential baking supplies, complete with brand-new, top-of-line baking sheets.

I looked at the shiny new pans. "These don't look like yours, Mom."

She laughed. "That's because mine are old and warped! These will bake evenly without burning!"

I couldn't argue. I didn't know how to articulate why the new ones just didn't have the same appeal, but I thanked her and continued to bake her prized cookies throughout my adult years.

Now, with a family of my own, I'm thankful for those times of comfort spent baking with my mom. The recipes I've learned from her have become such an important part of a love passed on to my own daughters. And I realize now why my shiny, new pans didn't evoke the same warm reassurance. They showed no marks of love. No time invested. Our "marred baking sheets" show that we have put many years of time and effort into passing love on.

I'm proud to say that my baking sheets are now as marked up as my mother's. And my daughters will soon be old enough to make cookies all on their own. That should give me more time to figure out how much milk to add . . .

Jaime Schreiner - Tisdale, Saskatchewan

THANKS FOR BEING

My Sunshine

Thank you, Mom, for finding in your wallet every year a spot for my school photo. Even in 8th grade, when my face was mostly dental work, you found a space. What a gift of confidence this gave me, just knowing in my goofy grin you took a little pride.

And even now, in my adulthood as I wait in grocery lines, it makes me smile to remember hidden deep within your wallet, you have aligned my face with opera stars on ticket stubs, your favorite cookie fortune, and that one-hundred-dollar bill you found in 1984.

Rachel Sprague - Seattle, WA

In 1968, I was in 2nd grade. We lived half a block from my elementary school, so I walked to school daily. At that time, parents could allow their children to walk to school without fear that any harm would come to them.

During this time, my mother worked the night shift at the local textile factory. She would generally get home from a long night's work at about 7:30 a.m., at which time she would either make my lunch or give me lunch money for the day and send me off to school.

On this particular rainy morning, unbeknownst to me, she'd had car trouble and was late getting home. We didn't have any lunch makings, so I went on to school without a lunch or money. I told my teacher about my dilemma, and she explained that I could charge my lunch and pay later.

At lunchtime, while I waiting in the lunch line, my mother showed up with a sack lunch. Upon arriving home, she had realized I must have gone to school without lunch or money. She had walked to the store, bought cold cuts, bread, and chips, walked home, made my lunch, and walked back to my school in the rain.

This is the first real memory I have of realizing how much my mother loved me and has taught me to love and raise my children in the same selfless way. Thanks, Mom!

Gloria Mulder - Yale, OK

Dear Mom,

I could not have made it through graduate school without you. The best part of the week? Your cards. Who else can say that they received a card from their mom every week that they were away. No matter what you had going on, you never skipped a week. Because of this, I have over 100 cards from you—all in a special box. 100 cards.

Thanks, Mom! I love you.

Love, Melissa

Melissa Borza - Dover, DE

Growing up we always went out of town for Christmas. Mom told us that Santa came early to our house because he knew. (Santa knows things like this.) We would all be in the car ready to go out for the evening, and Mom would forget something and run back in the house. Little did we know she went back inside to fill our stockings and get our gifts ready early.

We would come home, walk in, and our mouths would drop open with the reality that Santa really did come early. He just always seemed to know our schedule. We didn't have a lot of money, but my sister and I never knew that. Mom always made sure we had a wonderful Christmas.

One of my best memories of Christmas was running into the living room and seeing a brand new doll sitting on top of her very own suitcase. My sister also had a similar doll sitting with her own luggage. What we didn't know was that inside each doll's case were handmade doll clothes. It must have taken Mom hours and hours to make all of these beautiful creations: dresses, slacks, tops, pajamas. We thought we were the luckiest girls in the world as we giggled with delight holding up each article of clothing for our new doll.

As it turns out, we were indeed very fortunate young ladies; we had a mom who made sure that we never realized we were short on money. After all, we had something much more valuable—the creative, dedicated love of a mom who refused to let anything stand in the way of making our holiday the best we could ever imagine.

I still think of that Christmas, the homemade beautiful clothes, the doll, the suitcase—but mostly Mother smiling ear to ear realizing all her time and effort was worth every stitch!

Cheryl Sands - Lee's Summit, MO

On a hot Saturday evening in July, my mom shared a secret with me. I was 10 years old at the time and very disappointed that I couldn't go camping with my brother and father. As soon as they left, she turned to me and said, "We are going to have a girls' night!" My mind raced with possibilities. What was a girls' night?

It was during the late 60s when my father expected a big dinner every evening, except on Sundays when we had a midday dinner with dessert. He also expected a clean house at all times. Toys stayed in the bedroom. Eating was in the dining room only, and we were always supposed to be dressed as if company were coming. But that Saturday, we had no rules.

My mom brought out floral caftans for us to wear that she had sewn herself. She put TV dinners in the oven and brought TV trays into the living room. When the aroma of crispy chicken filled our house, she placed the dinners on the trays, and we ate them right out of the aluminum containers. I marveled at how mixed vegetables, mashed potatoes, and even apple cobbler could be cooked all at once with no pots or pans to wash later.

Afterwards, she set up a card table in the living room and poured out a 500-piece jigsaw puzzle picturing kittens playing with balls of yarn. We ate salty chips and walnut fudge brownies and drank sodas while working the puzzle. And when we spilled or dropped crumbs, we just laughed and said it'll keep 'til Sunday.

For one whole night, we were ladies of leisure doing as we pleased. After our favorite variety TV shows went off, my mom put records on the stereo, and we danced every popular move we knew until way past midnight. Later, we made popcorn on the stovetop and watched the late, late show.

By Sunday afternoon, prior to my father and brother returning, we had cleaned the house, put dinner on the table, and no one was the wiser. But every so often, I'd glance at my mom, and we would exchange smiles about our secret. Thank you, Mom, for my very first girls' night.

Linda Hullinger - Montgomery, TX

Dear Mom,

When I was seven, each Saturday you'd wake me early. We'd plant Gramps in his easy chair with his coffee and biscuits. He was blind then. As he swatted our crazy parrot swirling over his head, we'd head downtown. Rain or snow, we'd bus down to the largest department store in Montreal! The big sale! We had to get a good place in line before the doors opened.

I laugh now. I was the only boy there, hand held by my mom, for crying out loud! When I spotted Jim's birdbrained sister smirking at me in that crowd of pushy women, I felt the red creep up my face! There would be heck to pay at school on Monday!

The double glass doors opened, and about fifty wild women flooded in. You'd grab a cart and push your way to Housewares. Within seconds, the neatly displayed merchandise looked like a tornado had hit! You frantically sorted through pots or towels, wrestling with ballistic females not as adept at this as you!

But it was just a drill for you! We both knew we couldn't afford to buy anything. We'd leave the store empty-handed. Exhilarated nonetheless, the cart left at the door, you'd take me home.

But once, instead of Housewares, you confused me and led me to Boys' Sportswear. You pulled out a red and blue jersey with matching shorts, the colors of my favorite hockey team.

Then, holy moly, you placed a black garter belt into our cart! This time we made it through checkout! Never again would I have to wear your PINK garter belt to hold up my hockey socks! Your argument had been, "Pink, shmink! So what? It holds up your socks!" Now, no more teasing from the boys at the rec center! This kid was thrilled!

The jersey and the shorts were cool! But the garter belt was tops! I still see the joy in your eyes as I thanked you. I even called you "Mommy!"

I have so much to thank you for, Mom. Who would have thought that this would stand out in my mind some sixty years later?

Thanks for the garter belt, Mommy. I still have it in a box somewhere.

Love,
Lawrence

Larry Carter - Dallas, TX

Our cat had a litter of kittens, and one of them had vanished. At Mom's urging, my sisters and I began a search across the farm. We looked everywhere—under the old car, in the trash can, behind the oak trees, around the swing set, but we came up empty-handed.

Mom told us not to give up, and that's when I heard it—a tiny squeak of a meow coming from the shed. I pushed the door open, and to my surprise, the kitten was sitting right by the door. I was pumped! I scooped him up, ran to Mom to show her, and she said, "You're a hero!"

That evening, she threw me a "Hero Party" and made chocolate cake to celebrate. Mom really did make four-year-old-me feel like a hero! But the truth is, now that I'm a dad, the twenty-eight-year-old-me realizes what a hero my mom is.

Mom, thank you for all you did for me growing up. Thanks for encouraging me to keep trying, for teaching me right from wrong, and for putting a little heroic flair in my step. I hope as a parent I can make my kids feel like heroes just like you did for me, but I might need to borrow your cape first!

Stuart Chapman - Boerne, TX

THANKS FOR BEING

My Inspiration

My mom has always told me that I could do anything I want to do, if I work hard enough to achieve it. She encouraged this and shaped in me an "overachiever" attitude ever since I was a young girl.

I remember when I was four years old; my mom was determined to teach me to write my first name before I started school. My name is longer than most, so we practiced writing it several times a day for weeks. She was so proud of all the hard work that we had put into mastering this skill. We'd "show off" for family and friends every chance we got, and that praise quickly created a need in me to express my artistic abilities.

By the time kindergarten started, I was able to print my full name and had "secretly" begun to learn to write my first name in cursive. I remember thinking that my name looked the prettiest this way, and before too long, my signature was perfected.

Eager to please my mom, I began to share my accomplishment with the rest of the family in various ways. Although my parents disagreed with me at the time, I happened to have thought that "Kim Berly" looked beautiful written on her walls and engraved into the front of my dresser drawer. In fact, I loved my handwriting so much, I grabbed an ink pen and lovingly carved my name into the back of my dad's new leather chair. It was a masterpiece, and by the smile on my mom's face, I knew that she loved it!

I'm thankful that my mom is a kind and GENTLE woman. I did receive a stern talking-to, but truly things could have turned out much worse for me "in the end!" Although she gave me permission to "do anything" I wanted to do, this wasn't quite what she had in mind.

I'm grateful that my mom finds the humor in moments like these and continues to cheer me on with everything I do. I want to thank my mom for recognizing great art, no matter where it may appear, and for encouraging me to work hard and grab hold of my dreams.

Kimberly Murray - Livonia, MI

Mom,

As I stood there, surrounded by my fellow graduates, I looked into the sea of onlookers for your face. And when I found it, I saw that you were looking back at me, with tears streaming down your smiling cheeks.

That was the moment when I knew that no matter what I did with my life, if I could be half the mother you are, I would be the most successful person standing on that stage.

Thanks, Mom.

Love,
Your Daughter

Theresa Whitehead - Arnold, MO

Each time I listen to a beating heart,
it reminds me of when I was small.
I remember you telling me, "You can do anything, if you try."
I knew I could do it all.

It was never an easy journey —
grueling exams, long hours, and stress.
But I knew you'd be there with me, Mom,
you would never give anything less.

You helped me pursue my lifelong wish
to help, to heal, and to cure.
I owe all my happiness and success to you,
of this I am quite sure.

So each time I place my stethoscope on a patient's chest
or reach out to shake their hand,
know that in the back of my mind I am thanking you, Mom,
for making me who I am.

Michelle Brosnan - Roslyn Heights, NY

Mom,

I know I was not always the daughter you deserved. I didn't always believe that you cared. There were so many times in our lives that I brushed off your attempts to get closer and many others where you tried to love and support me, but I wouldn't let you in.

Perception is a funny thing. Two people can see the exact same thing and perceive it so differently. I once thought I didn't need you and was glad to have it that way. My perception of you was one of a woman who had no backbone, no conviction, and no courage. I was wrong.

There were times I was making choices and decisions (many not so good) about my life, on my own—you were there, watching, waiting, and loving me.

I was a belligerent daughter, stubborn and insisting on my own way even at the expense of my family. Once, I left the house for months, staying in the city and claiming to quit school, not speaking to you to prove a point. But always checking on things through secret (I thought they were) calls to sis.

Even after I had children of my own, I still carried the same perception of you. In my head, I had myself convinced that I was going to be a much better, completely different mother than you were. You were there every time I needed you, though. When I split from the kids' dad, you were there to help me whenever I asked. And I asked a lot. Over time, I saw it—the love, the strength, the courage.

At first it came through the eyes of my children. Oh, how they both loved time at Mee-maw and Popo's house! Initially, I was jealous of the way they behaved for you and rebelled at home. But eventually, my perception changed, again.

Mom, we have been through so much and always together. Even though I wouldn't admit it back then, you were a source of strength for me through so many challenging times. And watching your love, courage, and dignity during Dad's illness and death was a source of pride for me! Today I can say that I pray I am as wonderful a mother as you are! Perception is a funny thing . . .

Brenda Hennigs - Elkhorn, NE

Dear Mom,

At 5, I was so shy, so afraid to be without you. You gave me confidence in who I was and showed me how to be brave. I went off to school knowing you really weren't that far away and felt confident. All because of you.

At 10, I was afraid to go on a field trip thinking I would be too far from home. You packed me the best activity bag there ever was, and I stayed busy the whole trip. I was proud that I had gone. All because of you.

At 18, I was crying about leaving home. You rocked me on your knee, yes, even at 18, and I gladly cuddled in, soaking in the safety, and the tears stopped. All because of you.

At 22, I received my degree, to follow in your footsteps as a teacher. You taught me to work hard. I walked across that stage proudly, knowing you were in the audience and accepted the scroll. All because of you.

At 24, you walked me down the aisle with Dad. I had found the man of my dreams, because you had instilled in me what to look for. I married the perfect one. All because of you.

At 28, I had to say goodbye to you. I wasn't ready. But you had taught me how to cope. I was able to continue in life, remembering the lifetime we had together, the wisdom you gave me, the love you showed me. All because of you.

And now, at 34, I am a mom. I wish you were here to see it. I think about all the things you taught me, did for me, showed me, and most of all, how you loved me. I am going to be a great mom. All because of you.

Thank you, Mom. I am who I am because of you.

Corrie

Corrie Kirk - Nipawin, Saskatchewan

When I was young and in 5th grade,
We did a classroom play.
I had to sing a solo
Plus had lots of lines to say.

"You'll be fine and you'll do great!"
My mom said with a grin.
"Just do your best and all the rest
Will work out, don't give in!"

So came the night, as I got dressed,
My robe made from some sheets.
My nerves were shot, my stomach turned,
But then, right there . . . my feet!

"Oh, my gosh, I have no shoes,
What am I gonna wear?"
And Mom, with a smile, gently said,
"My dear, they're over there."

I quickly grabbed the box she'd placed
Lying on its side.
I opened it with shaky hands,
My smile became wide!

My mom had bought some fancy shoes,
They glittered and did shine.
"When you sing, just feel my love,
And you will do just fine!"

So I sang and did my thing.
The play was lots of fun.
The nerves and shakes had gone away,
I felt like I had won!

At first I thought my fancy shoes
Had helped me through the play.
But then, of course, it dawned on me,
It was much, much more that day.

Beyond the glam and sequins,
A message I would need,
"You're not alone . . . I am right here,
You're great and you'll succeed."

She knew just what I needed,
'Cause that's just how moms are.
They're always there and share their love,
To each of them . . . we're stars!

So thanks for "fancy shoes," dear Mom,
And everything you do.
Your love is always there for me.
I'll always love you, too!

Mar Sension - Altoona, PA

Hi, Mom; it's me, your oldest daughter.

You are now in a nursing facility and don't quite realize it because of dementia. But one thing it cannot take away from you is your love of your family and people.

My last visit, you still remembered me, asked what I had been doing, asked about the family, didn't want me to be overdoing it, and then left me to talk to your new friends. I got a smile on the inside and on my face at that.

Still the social butterfly! You were busy hovering over and advising some other residents—just like you do your own loved ones. That's you; that's my mother. Taking charge as usual. When a resident tried to escape, setting the alarm off, you asked, "What do you think you're doing?" The aide came out, directing him to his room; but I know it was that strong voice of yours that really got his attention.

After our visit, it was time to go; there you were, walking me to the elevator, telling me to be careful, making sure I had on enough clothes, and giving me that hug that only Mom can give, telling me you love me.

There's something about a mother's love. It is unstoppable; not even dementia can take it away. Your love transcends everything!

Love you back. See you soon.

Cheri Heath - Chicago, IL

When I was nine years old, Mama became interested in taxidermy. One day, she and I drove to town to get a few groceries. On the way back, we came across a coon lying in the road. It was obviously a fresh kill because it hadn't been there when we passed by 30 minutes or so before. After taking a good look at it and seeing that it didn't really have any damage to its fur, she decided to take it home and mount it.

Since we were in the car, this presented something of a problem. She didn't want to put the coon in the car and she didn't want to leave it. So, my mother, the woman who birthed me, turned and looked at me and said, "Here, hold this out the window."

I immediately shrank back in the car seat, shaking my head no. But Mama didn't take no for an answer. With shaking fingers, I grabbed the nasty thing and held on for dear life.

Coons might look all nice and fluffy, but that sucker weighed about ten pounds, and holding ten pounds of dead weight, pardon the pun, out the window is not as easy as it sounds, especially going 30-40 miles per hour.

All the way home, I kept readjusting my grip so that I wouldn't drop it on the highway. We finally made it home and I let it slither to the ground. My mother proceeded to mount it and "Rocky" graced our living room for a couple of years.

One day, Mama and I stopped at a Cracker Barrel in Tennessee for breakfast. As she was purchasing a toy for one of her grandkids, I found a basket that contained, of all things, a stuffed coon. I couldn't resist. She was taking her change when I walked up to her with the stuffed coon by the tail and said, "Here, hold this!"

Thanks, Mama, for making me the odd yet well-rounded woman I am!

Tricia Foster - Omaha, UT

THANKS FOR BEING

My

Reflection

When I look at myself
in the bathroom mirror
And instead see a reflection of you,
I don't roll my eyes and sigh with despair
Over the lady I've grown into.
Instead I smile and think to myself
That I'm thrilled with who I've become,
'Cause the best part of who I am today
Is the part that's just like you, Mom.

Thanks, Mom . . .
For all you've taught me . . .
For all you've encouraged me . . .
For all the me that is you.

Lynne Hayes - Mission Hills, KS

I've got to tell you something.
I'll write it in this letter.
It's haunted me three decades now.
That gray angora sweater.

I bet you rode the 'L' train
and fought the Christmas crowd.
You marched your way up State Street
as snow was being plowed.

You stopped to hear the jingle
of a frosty Christmas carol
then climbed the marble stairs
to Marshall Field's apparel.

I bet you searched a hundred racks
and knelt down on your knees
to rifle through the bottom shelf
of silk and soft chemise.

You tossed aside the cardigans.
And corduroy. For better.
Until you found the perfect gift.
That gray angora sweater.

I loved my Christmas sweater.
I wore it everywhere.
That fuzzy-wuzzy fabric.
That furry bunny hair.

I wasn't very worldly
but somehow I knew still,
you bought that comfy sweater
with your only crumpled bill.

That's why I felt my heart break
that awful fateful day
when I smoothed my gray angora
in a soft and caring way.

Then, I misted it so gently
with the lightest water wisp,
before I pressed my iron down
and burnt it to a crisp!

I hadn't even thanked you yet.
So what was I to say?
I'd taken it for granted
like the things you did each day.

I hid my guilty feelings
and the thank-you left unsaid,
like the charred, discarded sweater
that I stuffed beneath my bed.

But yesterday, I saw your face.
It smiled from my locket
as I found a smashed banana peel
inside my child's pocket.

I realized that I'm overdue.
It's time to thank you now
for all the selfless things you did
to make life full somehow.

For every little kindness
like homemade chocolate chips.
For summer swims and card games
and sunset picnic trips.

For teaching me to read and write
and multiply by threes.
For shoelace bows and folded clothes
and practice spelling bees.

For chicken soup and Kleenex.
For training wheels unscrewed.
For weathering tornados
from every teenage mood.

For loving me through all of it.
For knowing I'd grow better.
And one day I would thank you for
that gray angora sweater.

Madeleine Kuderick - Palm Harbor, FL

Dear Mom,

I remember you telling me stories of my birth when I was a small child. You were so happy that I was a girl! You told me that you cried, and I asked you why. The next words out of your mouth were ones that have meant a lifetime of love. You told me you cried because it hurt, but mostly because I was just the one you wanted.

You have continuously marked the events of my life with those words. Birthdays, dance recitals, basketball games, breakups, graduations, my wedding, and the birth of my sweet baby boy were all met with those words. "You are just the one I wanted."

I know I've been far from a perfect daughter, but I've never once doubted your love for me. That is a blessing not everyone has.

In my early 20s, I remember discussing the fear of turning into your mother with my friends. After I got married and had my own child, I realized I AM like you, and I'm beyond proud of that fact.

You taught me to follow my dreams and supported me when I decided to become a teacher (just like you). You showed me how to be a wife and mother with the little, everyday things you'd do or say in between the big life events that everyone keeps track of. You sacrificed your time, energy, and personal goals to help me with mine. I had your unconditional love even when I didn't deserve it. I hope to share that kind of love with my own children.

I can't imagine my life without you, Mom. You're just the one I wanted, too.

Love,
Becca

Rebecca Kyle - Dripping Springs, TX

Dear Mom,

I think I'm catching up to you.

Oh, sure you can still outshop me, outwalk me, and Lord knows, outtalk me. Your legs are much nicer than mine, and there's not a jowl in sight. The dreaded jowl that droops like melted candle wax above a saggy double chin . . . but I digress.

Yes, I am catching up to you. My hair is gray, I lose my car keys, I call my children by their other siblings' names. When I lodge a complaint, I take it straight to the "big nachos'" just like you. (But doesn't everyone?) I can match you drink by drink, as long as it stops at two. Like you, I get upset when I can't taste the coconut in my strawberry daiquiris, proof that there is no alcohol in them! It's a flat-out conspiracy!

I am 51 years old, and I still lay my head on your shoulder when I'm sick, and you make me soup and Jell-O. I may get sick more than anyone you know . . . but I really, really like soup and Jell-O! When you are sick, I always bring you cold soda and those nasty marshmallow and chocolate cakes with goop in the middle that you love. Truthfully, I'm beginning to get suspicious whenever you cough or sneeze in my general direction.

Yes . . . I'm catching up to you. I own a huge pillbox that holds a small pharmacy, and I've discovered the epiphanies of prune juice. You've taught me how to make homemade noodles, and I've taught you not to overcook the roast. You've set the example for being a grandma, and now that I'm a grandmother, too, I understand that the best grandmas always put some pork on a fork and are never, ever fat. There is only more to love.

Thanks, Mom. I owe everything I am to you. I may be catching up to you . . . but you'll always win. When you are 74 with flawless legs, it's the rule.

Love (and envy),
Annette

P.S. **cough cough**

Annette Robidoux - Fruitport, MI

Four angels, our halos were held up by horns
You loved us in spite of our obvious thorns

Bickering, fighting, quibbles galore
We drove you quite batty, your offspring of four

"She's touching me, Mom!""I can't find my shoe!"
You just couldn't wait until we all grew

"Wait 'til your father gets home!" you would yell
That threat was enough, our antics to quell

We thought the "dad threat" was really your worse
We should have feared you and your horrible curse!

"I wish you a half dozen just like yourself!"
"Gee thanks, Mom, that's awesome, 'cause I love myself!"

We may have been brats, your authority tested
But aren't you glad, Mom, we were never arrested?

Up and out of your nest we since all have flown
Your offspring of four now have nests of our own

In your eyes, your grandchildren can do no wrong
You're amused by their "antics" all the daylong

"They are just being children," you calmly advise
"Enjoy them now, Dear, because time quickly flies"

One thing I must ask–my surprise I can't smother–
Who are you and what have you done with my mother?

As you sit there just grinning, I hear myself say:
"Just wait 'til your father gets home today!"

"Stop running! Don't fight! Leave your brother alone!
I just cannot wait 'til you children are grown!"

"And someday, you little mischievous elves,
I wish you each a half dozen just like yourselves!"

Shake my head with a sigh as you giggled with glee
It only took three, Mom. It only took three.

Looking back there aren't enough thanks I can give
For your role model, Mom (and for letting me live!)

So thank you, dear Mom, your "curse" was a blessing
My three are now grown, and I find it distressing

How quickly they grew, you were right—the time flew
I can't wait to have grandkids to cuddle and coo

And when they are driving MY children insane
I'll sit by and smile and calmly proclaim

"They are just being children," then I'll gently advise,
"Enjoy them now, Dear, because time quickly flies."

Donna Anderson - Frisco, TX

Mom,

Remember when I was young and I knew everything? You were such a control freak! You layered me in thick, ugly winter clothes, as if warmth trumped fashion. You dictated my every move, corrected my behavior, and shoved outdated morals down my throat, along with vitamins and repulsive vegetables. You swore one day I'd thank you. I laughed.

I was about twenty when I finally noticed wisdom in those once clueless eyes of yours. Suddenly, you had brilliant, useful input when I grudgingly asked your opinion. You stunned me by knowing a lot about life. The older I got, the smarter you seemed to grow. I actually took your advice when you weren't looking.

When I became a mom myself, you wowed me with your knowledge on kids. Where did you learn about timeouts, hiding medicine in applesauce, and stern, unwavering stares for tantrums? How did you know that I needed a hug when my son said he hated me for making him wear mittens and a scarf? Was it instinct that guided you to my door on his first solo car ride? How did you guess that I'd pace until he got home safely? Did you read a book on parenting? Did you sense the gratitude in my heart?

Last week, I found myself studying you at a family dinner. You laughed when your grandson griped about the vegetables, and I noticed, with poignant sadness, how old you've gotten. Your hands shook a little reaching for your glass, the fingers twisted with the arthritis you dismissively mentioned having. Thick lenses replaced the reading glasses you occasionally wore. Your back wasn't as straight as I remembered. My son muttered something about his ancient, grumpy teacher, a lady two years my senior. I chastised him softly, and your warm, empathic glance met mine across the table. I realized that I sounded just like you used to and that I was proud of that. I mouthed a heartfelt "thank you" across the table. Your eyes, which I now realize had always brimmed with wisdom and love, told me it was all you ever needed to hear.

Marya Morin - Saint-Lin–Laurentides, Quebec

One of the most wonderful gifts my mother has given me wasn't wrapped in shiny paper and didn't cost a cent. You see, my mom was a talker. She didn't care who you were or if she ever met you before. Mom would strike up a conversation with anyone and would talk and talk much to the recipient's delight. My mom made every conversation interesting and fun! A shy friend would soon be chatting, and strangers would start sharing their life adventures. My mom brought the best out in everyone! She often joked that she "would talk to a wall if it could listen!"

As a young child, I was painfully shy. I was an observer, never a participant; oftentimes people would ask me if the cat got my tongue. I wanted so badly to join in the fun at birthday parties or raise my hand in class because I knew the answer. Since I was an observer, I also watched my mom. I saw her engaged in all fun activities, laughing, and conversing. She was the life of the party.

I don't know how it happened, but it did. I brought home my report card when I was in the fourth grade, and there in bold letters the teacher scrawled, "Dorann needs to quiet down in class. She's become quite the chatterbox." Imagine that, me a chatterbox! That was the best report card ever! My mom just smiled, and we gave each other a knowing look, like mother like daughter!

As I stand on the checkout line at the grocery store and strike up a conversation with the person in front of me, my son asks, "Do you have to talk to everyone, Mom?"

My answer is, "Yes I do and I would talk to a wall if it could listen."

Thank you, Mom, for the gift of gab!

Dorann Weber - Brown Mills, NJ

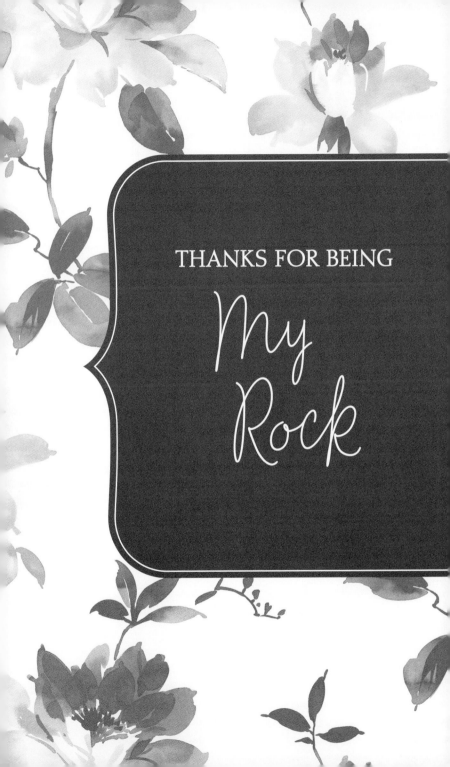

THANKS FOR BEING

My
Rock

When you first came upon us three
What a change there was going to be
We were mere scraps scattered about
Still beautiful and filled with color—no doubt
But we were terribly lacking
Our filling, our threads, and our backing
You took us, those mere scraps
Against your intentions perhaps
And brilliantly, devotedly fashioned
The most valuable quilt imagined
Bound together with love and devotion
We prove the eternal notion
That quilts come from scraps long forgotten
And like these colorful pieces of cotton
A perfect patchwork called family was rebuilt
We owe it to the first one you ever made—The Quilt

Kristin Boone - Fairmont, WV

I'm thankful you stood by my side

To dry all the tears that I cried.

Your comfort, dear Mother,

Is matched by no other,

Though ice cream comes close,

I'll confide.

Armanda Liedke - Windham, ME

Dear Mom,

The sadness in your eyes walking away from the coffin at the wake was more than I could bear. Where has the time gone?

A sudden flash of memories hit me like a brick. Dad was a good father to all of us, and I never once saw him treat you or any of us wrong. But you were always there. You didn't leave us to go work out of town or have to apologize for missing a school play. You were never too tired to make us costumes on Halloween or make hot cocoa and homemade donuts.

You once told me that one day I would realize just how the small, little things in life would become the most treasured. It breaks my heart to see you in pain, and I only wish I could comfort you, as you have for so many countless times in my life.

I remember at age seven, I wrecked my bike and Dad was upset, but you tended the cut on my head and the scrapes on my hands. You even blamed that dumb old bicycle.

At age twelve, I quit my paper route and was afraid to tell you. For weeks, I would still get up and leave the house so you wouldn't know, but you did.

Mr. Sanders called you the very day I quit. But you somehow knew I would come to see you sooner or later. It took me just over four weeks. You held my face with your loving hands and looked me in the eyes. Your only words were, "There's more to life than throwing papers, Son." I was so relieved.

At age eighteen, my best friend passed away. I was so hurt and had experienced for the first time in my life what true loss felt like. I came to you, and still this day, you comforted me.

I search for the words to tell you how sorry I am for your loss, your love for so many years. Again you hold my face in your hands and tell me you are fine and for me to remember to honor my father and how proud he was of me.

You are so right about the little things, Mom, but you are wrong about one thing: you are the most treasured thing in my life. I will always and forever love you.

Your loving son,
Tommy

Thomas Gilbert - Santa Fe, TX

"Are you pregnant?" you ask.
"Yes," I reply.

This would normally be
a happy, joyous occasion.
One when people ask,
"How are you feeling?"
"When are you due?"
"That's so exciting!"
"I am happy for you . . ."

I am sixteen.
Instead, I wait
for the yelling and tears
to begin,
but they don't.

Silence follows.
More silence
follows the silence.
Forever goes by
before words are found.

"Have you been to the doctor?"
"Yes."
"When is your next appointment?"
"Tuesday after school."
"I will pick you up."
"You don't have to."
"I want to."
"OK."
More silence.

"I love you, Sweetheart."
"I love you, too, Mom . . ."

Exhale . . .
Tears . . .

Moving forward
through a pregnancy
with disapproving looks
and unkind words,
I see how much
you care
as you stand beside me
in the delivery room,
happily awaiting
the arrival of your
grandchild.

Eighteen years go by.

I look at my baby all grown up
and begin to understand
the depth of love and support
that was there
when I needed it most.

I realize how great you are today
but would like to say, "Thank You, Mom"
for all the yesterdays.

Eileen Reese - Hague, Saskatchewan

Mom,

You're my everything. I can't begin to tell you how much I love you.

Four years ago, you moved me into my first dorm at college. My freshman year was one of the hardest times of my life—between a dramatic breakup to getting really sick and always in and out of doctors' offices . . . But through all that, we became best friends.

I don't know what I would have done without you. I'm SO incredibly lucky to have such a great mom, who drives an hour and a half every other day for me when I'm upset or who takes me shopping or to get my nails done when I'm overwhelmed and stressed with school.

I get so frustrated with being so sick sometimes and having to do more tests and go see more doctors, but you've always been there . . . sitting right next to me. You hold my hand when I cry, help me clean my apartment when my roommate destroys it and send me little gifts on holidays like Valentine's Day when I'm the only one without a boyfriend . . .

You make my dreams come true, no matter how distant they seem. I got to see Blink 182 front row in New York, I've been to Europe (with you!), and soon, I'll be moving to New York City. All because YOU believe in me.

I started running again, and to see you at the finish line cheering me on brings back memories from middle and high school. I don't think you've ever missed a race or a soccer game. I'm spoiled rotten, but I want you to know how much I appreciate everything you do for me and how much you've given up to make my life as incredible as it is. You know you're pretty awesome if I'd rather go on a trip with you for my 21st birthday rather than any of my friends! Ha!

Thank you for being you. And for loving me. You're the best mom I could ever ask for. I'll always be here for you.

I love you.

Megan McAuliffe - Greensboro, NC

Dear Mom,

Sometimes I secretly believe you are a superhero. I look back on how you were able to raise three kids, well, four including Dad, and keep it all together.

I think of how you decided to keep your career as a hairdresser so our family would have enough money, but wanted to also be there for us kids, so you made your beauty salon connected to our house.

I remember when I was younger, I just expected things to be a certain way or to be done because you just always did them. Like every morning when I woke up to go to school, you made time before work to cook all three of us kids breakfast and made sure my side ponytail was curled and in place and Dad's hair was perfectly combed to the right side.

I remember coming home off the bus and you being there ready to greet me with a hug, as you matched your last appointment to the end of our school day just to be there with us.

I think of all the countless dinners you prepared, the endless laundry that you did, and the unconditional love you gave to the boys and me!

I think about the nights you stayed up with us when we were sick and how you would come to each of our bedsides for our nightly prayers and sing us a lullaby. I still, to this day, do not know how you were able to do all of those things and so many more.

Mom, I can never thank you enough for everything you have done for our family and me. You truly are a superhero and, more importantly, my hero! I love you!

Love,
Bridget

Bridget Fullerton - Toledo, OH

I remember it was raining that day, and I was calling from a payphone in the front of a laundromat.

"Hi, Mom." I struggled to be understood through the sobbing. "I got fired."

"What! What happened?" she asked.

"I don't know!" I said somewhat forcefully. Then, trying very hard to take a deep breath, I looked across the street at the office I had just been asked to leave. "I came in this morning, and the boss said that I was doing good work but he just couldn't afford to keep me around."

"He got let go," I heard her whisper to my dad.

I still, to this day, don't know what he said in response, but there was silence on the line for about five seconds while my mom and I searched for more words. And I'll never forget her statement that broke the silence: "Go get a haircut."

That made me laugh.

"Get a haircut, have lunch, and see a movie. Then tomorrow, you'll look for something else."

In retrospect, I guess my mom had worked my whole life to teach me about focusing on the things that really matter and not letting temporary setbacks slow me down. But at that moment, I felt the weight of the world crashing down around me, and she reached out over a hundred miles to gently pull me out from under it. For that, I will always be grateful.

Judah Rosenstein - Elkins Park, PA

Dear Mom,

March 10, 1981, was a day that changed my life and one that, unfortunately, changed yours, too. The car accident left me with two broken knees and months of healing and rehabilitation.

Your life changed that day as well. Your days were no longer your own, and your responsibilities were now tied to my care. You did it all with love and never once made me feel like a burden.

You held my hand when I needed your touch, you took care of my needs, and even when everyone else was sound asleep, you were only steps away from me.

As I look back, I realize that your love for me was so much bigger than I ever realized or imagined. I know I was not the best patient, and I am sure I tried your patience on many occasions.

I want to say THANK YOU from the bottom of my heart. You are a wonderful mom, and your love carried me when I could not walk. You have made me the woman I am today, and I am so very proud of you.

Love,
Karen

Karen Messick - Statesville, NC

You had five little rug rats
In a span of seven years
A full-time job to say the least
With little praise or cheers

Some days were like gymnastics
All artistry and grace
But most days found us freestyle
More like a downhill race

You high-jumped over piles of clothes
With scarcely any fuss
You made the hundred-meter dash
To help us catch the bus

The curling was done on your little girls' hair
For church each Sunday morning
While the boys were always horsing around
Despite your many warnings

You used your expert diving skills
To catch us when we'd fall
The score I'd give for your quick moves
Would be the best of all

You wiped our tears and calmed our fears
Your torch of love burned pure
If medals came with motherhood
You'd get the gold for sure

Sheree Knighton - Newton, NC

My mom has always been my biggest fan, in life as well as in sports.

I have played soccer all my life at a highly competitive level; however, throughout all this time my mom has still not learned the game. No matter how well or how awful my team played, my mom always thought we played a great game! Whenever a call went against our team, no matter the reason, she always thought the referees were wrong.

My mom is also quite a vocal lady. During a high school game, I was fouled, and then I heard a voice from the stands yelling the loudest and longest sentence I had ever heard. In it, she included who had fouled me, what she did to foul me, how wrong the refs were for not making a call, and that I was her daughter and she didn't appreciate the foul being committed.

Instead of being embarrassed or mad that my mom had made all this noise—and everyone on the field could hear her—I was proud. I looked at the girl next to me from the opposing team, smiled, and just said, "That's my mom." She looked at me and rolled her eyes.

I ran away and played the rest of the game with a smile on my face. I knew at that moment that no matter what was going on in my life, she would always have my back.

Andrea VanWashenova - Canton, MI

Mom,

I may not have been the beauty queen, the athlete, or the golden child that my siblings were. But, I always knew that you loved me. The klutzy, chubby one who tried really hard, but never actually succeeded in being great at anything.

You struggled right alongside of me as we tried to find my niche in life. Patiently teaching me to tie my shoes "bunny ear style" when I couldn't manage the "over, under, and through" way. Driving me to and from practices, lessons, and miscellaneous group meetings. You were always there cheering me on, celebrating my successes, and consoling me through my defeats.

You were my advocate when the school system attempted to label me with "special needs." And then again, when I was diagnosed with not one, but three different diseases. You never let anyone—including myself—treat me any differently than anyone else. The words "pity party" weren't in our vocabulary.

We took things day by day and made them work. We "looped and conquered" each roadblock we came up against. Found something good about every day, even if we had to make that good thing up. Sometimes it was something as silly as, "At least I didn't drop my toothbrush in the toilet today" or as big as, "I finally found something I'm really good at!"

Thank you for teaching me that it's OK not to be perfect. That it's OK to laugh at myself. And that all boys that age are jerks! Your continued love and support have made me who I am today. And for that, I am eternally grateful.

Joelle Beebe - Midland, MI

Dear Mom,

Growing up physically disabled, I depended heavily on you. You took care of my bathing and dressing. You took me to high school and wheeled me to my classes until I found kids who would wheel me. For 20 years, you drove me to work. You first learned to drive in order to take me to school. You would lift me into the car and fold up and lift my wheelchair into the trunk. Even though driving a van frightened you, when I got my motorized chair you learned how to drive one because the chair could not be folded.

You made incredible sacrifices for me and spent your life putting my needs first. You always worried about who would stay with me whenever you went out, and for years, you and Dad couldn't go away together. I remember times calling you to my job because I needed to use the bathroom, and you would leave your job.

I know you would say that you did what any mother would do for her child, especially one with special needs, but that's not necessarily true. You did a job that was above and beyond the call of duty.

I'm sure you shed many tears over my pain. You took me to doctors and hospitals trying to find a treatment or a possible cure only to hear bad news. I know you cried not only for yourself but for me as well. I can only imagine how devastating it must be for a parent to have a disabled child knowing there's no cure.

Because I've always lived with you and for the special care you've given me, we have a special relationship. You have been my mother and my friend. We have confided in each other on many occasions.

As a disabled woman, I was often treated as a child by many people, but you always treated and respected me as an adult. Even though I'm married now and have Bob with me every night and a health aide every day, I still need you. I still need to talk to you, and at times, I need someone to stay with me. You've always been there for me.

Thank you for being a friend, a confidante, a caregiver, and so much more. Thank you for being my mother.

Love,
L

Linda Manning - Cedarhurst, NY

Dearest Mom,

How did you do it?!

How were you able to live, love, and learn with six kids, one dog, a mother-in-law, and her traditional baby boy?

How did you make time to attend every PTA meeting, volunteer in the school office, help us with our homework, drive us to school when we missed the bus—all this with one car?

How did you keep track of us when one was at dance practice, the other at piano lesson, yet another cheerleading, one at fencing practice and who knows where the other two were even though there were no cell phones?

How did you remain calm when we broke dishes while washing them or the whining of the little ones because the bigger ones were teasing them or the disapproving expressions from Grandmom because she would not have done something the way you did?

How did you laugh at one's silliness, discipline one's naughtiness, accept one's bashfulness, deal with one's talkativeness, embrace one's moodiness, hug one's tearfulness, and protect one's recklessness while at the same time loving all of the craziness that made us a family—and this was before cable TV?

How did you keep us quiet in the evening so that Daddy could sleep before working the graveyard shift and then coming home to go to another full-time job in the morning?

You are my role model, my mentor, and I am so grateful that the Lord gave us His very best!

Valerie

Valerie Aleksandruk - Norristown, PA

THANKS FOR BEING

My
Everything

As a mom of six,
it's not surprising folks would say,
"Are you on a field trip?"
on any given day.
And a teacher's statement
could always make you grin:
"You're another Mathews kid?
Please, do come in!"

With pride, prayer, and patience . . .
and a little help from Dad,
You've raised six unspoiled, non-bratty kids,
though moments we have had!
Thank you, Mom, for loving us
and providing a well-balanced start
To live a life that emulates
your awesome, caring heart.

Marcia Dutschmann - Hewitt, TX

Mom,

I'm not sure where or when we lost the ability to say, "I love you." Probably somewhere between the fact that we're not mushy people, nor are we gonna be the first to say it! I feel it though. I feel it in your actions. I feel it in the way you treat me. I have felt your love for as long as I can remember. And for the times before I can remember, I have my baby book. I have flipped through those pages reading the words "I love her so much" a million times over.

I want to thank you for pouring your heart out in your writing. I feel, understand, and am completely overwhelmed by those words so much more now that I'm a mommy. And when you tell my babies that you love them, I know it's also meant for me. And if we never say it to each other, I hope you feel my love for you.

Love,
Summer

Summer Ruegger - Sandy, OR

You're the Thelma to my Louise,
The Laverne to my Shirley.
You cheer me on in all I do
Even when I get a little squirrelly!

You're the best friend
A daughter could ask for.
We've had super adventures
With many more in store.

Whether we're on the road
Not sure where to go
Or trying to hit the jackpot
At our favorite casino.

Whenever I need you,
You're there by my side.
I can count on you
Every inch of the ride.

Thanks to you, Mom,
You are my best friend,
And it will stay that way
To the Very End!

Paula Mortimer - Chilton, WI

Mom,

I never imagined that when I joined the military I would also be leaving behind a mother who loves me dearly. I know it must have broken your heart and left the house in silence. I can imagine you sitting alone at the table drinking coffee or flipping through the channels just to try and find a way to not think about me being gone.

Both of us have had to adjust in our own way. I have grown up quite a bit now, and my appreciation for you and the sacrifices you have made for me grows daily as I mature.

I've been gone for nearly 7 years now. I'm sure you think your baby girl is gone forever, but I'm not. I'll ALWAYS come back to you, and no matter what, you will always have the biggest piece of my heart. Thank you for always supporting me and wanting the best for me, even if it may have caused you some grief.

I love you, MOM!

Elisa Sinclair - Chesapeake, VA

We don't hug, we don't kiss,
we show no physical forms of affection.
It's uncomfortable, all that lovey-dovey stuff,
we don't need that kind of connection.

You kept me fed and raised me right,
surely that's love enough.
And in return, here's a "Thanks, Mom"
without all the fluff.

Bennie Newsome - Birmingham, AL

Dear Mom,

As an infant, you were my fuzzy blanket, my peaceful lullaby, and my worn rocking chair.

As a child, you were my chicken noodle soup, my double-checked homework, and my stuffed Rainbow Brite lunchbox.

As a teenager, you were my neatly pressed dress, my familiar cheer from the stands, and my front porch light.

As a college student, you were my timely care package, my home-cooked meal, and my happy holiday.

Today, you are my how-to book, my fortune cookie, and my rose-colored glasses.

With thanks for every little thing,
Your loving daughter

Bevin Reinen - Virginia Beach, VA

THANKS FOR BEING

My
Angel

Dear Mama,

It's been almost 7 years now since you left us, but hardly a day goes by that I don't think about you.

I open my desk drawer at work and there is the little red devotion book you gave me over 20 years ago. It's dog-eared and tattered but still read often. It is full of lessons I know you wanted me to learn. But the best lessons learned are the ones you taught me:

Never feel sorry for myself; if I can't look around and see someone worse off than I am, I need to look harder, because they are certainly there.

There is nothing I can't accomplish with determination and hard work. And if I do fail, at least I know it isn't for lack of trying.

Love deeply and unconditionally. You used to tell me that no one loved their children more than you and Daddy did. At the time, I thought that was a strange thing to say; everyone loves their children. But as I've grown, I've come to realize you were right; there is nothing that you and Daddy wouldn't have done for us. And this is the same love I carry in my heart for my own family.

Just the other day, my 3-year-old grandson and I were looking through my photo album, and there he was—a wrinkled, red-faced newborn being held by your hands. I had to look twice to realize they were actually my hands. I am proud of these hands that look like yours; these hands reach out every night to touch the man I have been married to for almost 38 years. They have held and rocked my own son, and now they hold my grandchildren.

Mama, my prayer is that as I grow old I will use these hands to guide my child and now my grandchildren and, with God's help, mold them into the strong, productive adults that you would want them to be. This is the legacy that I want to pass along to future generations that may come into our family. Who knows? Maybe someday my granddaughter will be baking an apple pie from your recipe and look down and see her grandmother's hands.

Thanks, Mama, for the hands (and the recipe)!

Linda Lindsay - East Wenatchee, WA

Dear Mom,

I so wanted to read your journals after you passed away, but hesitated because they were your private thoughts. I thought it would be too painful for me to read. So this year, 5 years and 11 months after you left us, I said I think it may be time.

Tentatively, I opened the first journal and started to read. I saw the familiar handwriting; the cute little drawings you added to the bottom of some pages made me giggle once again at your humor. I got to about the third or fourth day from the beginning and read:

Rain Sunday 10:00 8/9/81
Kids got here about 1:00 this morning—
Lark is a cutie
Full by 4:30 new record
I got to say hi to Scott today he called Gina—lonesome I guess—Bless his heart—
Tracy looks good—Wish I could show how glad I am to see her—Maybe she will read this some day & know.
Hi Trace-D-Race
Night :)

I guess my decision to read your diaries was a good one. I continue to marvel at your compassion for everyone and every living thing through the tears and smiles—Thank you.

Trace-D-Race

Tracy Windsor - Douglasville, GA

As a child I had a wish list
Coming from my heart to you
Though I'm all grown-up now
I want to make sure you knew

The things that I would wish for you
I'm putting in this letter
All the fancy things the world has now
Could have made your life much better

You scrubbed clothes on a washboard
It looked so very hard
Then hanging them one by one on a line
That was stretched across the yard

You finally got a wringer washer
Though old, would have to do
I would wish you had an electric one
That was brand spankin' new

You wore your tattered dresses
Though thankful for them all
I would wish you had nice frilly ones
With a matching sweater for fall

You did your cooking on a woodstove
That only held one loaf of bread
I would wish for a double oven
So you would always be a loaf ahead

You were wonderful at sewing
Mending my clothing that I tore
I would wish for a lot of gift cards
So you could go shopping inside the store

You loved your artificial pearls
Lying softly in your drawer of socks
I would wish you had the expensive ones
With an actual jewelry box

You hoed the garden, pulled the weeds
In every single row
Wiping the sweat and rubbing your back
I knew it hurt you so

So a gardener would be another wish
For hoeing, weeding, and such
So you could enjoy your summer
Without working quite so much

You always had a love for growing things
Nurturing your plants and flowers
I'd wish for plenty of daylight
So you could admire them for hours

Your smile was like the sunshine
So warm and all so bright
When you'd slap your knee and laugh out loud
You'd seem to time it just right

You were such a blessing
I wanted you to know
You were my second mama
I wished you hadn't had to go

The last wish that I have
Well, it's kind of more for me
It's to hold you in my arms once more
But I know it just can't be

I miss you very much
I still cry a tear or two
If my wish comes true for an extra day
I would spend it loving you

Deana Scott - Quincy, IN

Mom,

I have never had the chance to say this since you died during my childbirth, but I look forward to the day in Heaven where I can say thank you for giving me life.

My aunts told me it was your choice going into the delivery that if a problem were to arise, I should be saved.

I hope as you looked down from Heaven all these years, I have not disappointed you and have done what you would have wanted me to.

Dad, as you know, remarried, and I must say my new mother always kept you in mind and made sure I shared events with your sisters and family. Although, when I was young, I never knew who they were exactly. Meaning, all my other aunts and uncles I could define to be on Dad's or Mom's side. I didn't know of you and your death until I was going into the service at 18. And, yes, it was my mom, or who I thought was my mom, who told me.

I think of you every day and pray to meet you in Heaven when I leave this earth. I truly believe you and the Blessed Mother have watched over and guided me as life went on, and I thank you.

Love,
Eddie

Ed Bracht - Elkton, FL

Mamaw,

As we were separated for 26 years by a closed adoption, I wanted you to know how much you touched me.

When I finally found you, you told me in your first letter that you always thought of me as your little princess. You told me that you and my mother always watched the little babies go by in the mall. You also told me that you had a fantasy that the handsome, young doctor who paid particular attention to my case after my surgery at birth had actually adopted me. I thought I was the only one with fantasies!

Thank you for the most special of words that had such an impact on my life. I love you and miss you deeply.

Your princess,
Theresa

Theresa Drinnon - Maryville, TN

Dear Mama,

Remember in 1986, the year after I got remarried and moved five hundred miles away, when my husband declared a $200 phone bill was not in our budget? That was also the year we began writing letters.

My letters, scribbled during naptimes, were about my husband's long hours at his new job, why babies tend to cut teeth at the same time their older siblings have ear infections, and about being so sleep-deprived that I once lost my good standing with the tooth fairy.

Your letters arrived with recipes for busy moms, coupons for diapers and baby detergent, and articles on how to get stains out. But they also came with words of encouragement to hang in there, things do get better, and the first years of marriage can be challenging, especially with a six-year-old child and a new baby.

Best of all, your letters brought me back home for a little while as you shared what was happening in your world: the meat loaf you'd cooked and how your homemade biscuits came out just right this time, the four-leaf clover you'd spotted on your way to the clothesline, and the bushel of corn that you'd shucked and frozen the day before.

I don't think I told you, but I made an event of your letters. I would not read a single word until I had quiet time, a fresh cup of coffee, and a sweet snack. Then I would read them as if they were the best novels ever.

After you passed away in 1997, I thought I'd gone through all of your things, but recently while cleaning out the attic, I found a box containing a brown fabric envelope that you'd sewn. Inside were my yellowed letters on assorted stationery and notebook paper.

Like mother, like daughter. I had kept all of your letters, too. I put them together, and every once in a while, I take one out and read it. Your letters comforted me back then, and they help me comfort my own daughter now.

Thank you, Mama, for giving me hope when I was down, for making me smile when I was sad, and for keeping me close in heart while I was far away.

Linda Hullinger - Montgomery, TX

If I had a penny for every time my mother said
"brush your teeth"
or "clean up your room" or "take a bath,"
then I'm pretty sure I'd have three or four
massive piggy banks filled to the brim.
It usually took more than one telling to get me to comply.
And I'm not sure why.

If I had a nickel for every time my mother said
I was the laziest girl she knew,
and I always figured she must have known a lot,
or that my face would freeze "that way,"
then I'd have at least six enormous piggy banks
full of those coins—
though my face never froze.

If I had a dime for every time mom said
something was wrong with my friends
and used that silly jumping-off-a-cliff line,
then another two piggies full of tenpence
would be mine.
Actually, given my adolescence, maybe four or five
banks would hold that change.
And some of those friends were not so nice.

If I had a quarter for every time my mom told me
to save myself for marriage,
another couple of large banks would hold most of them,
I think.
I know she meant saving in the physical sense,
but some parts of my soul
were saved for marriage.
I didn't think she was right about that,
but she probably was.

If I had a dollar for every time my mom said,
"I hope I live long enough to see your kids
and how they treat you,"
I'd have several lockboxes filled with lucky bucks.
She didn't live long enough to find out
that my kids treat me pretty much like I treated her.

If I had all those pennies, nickels, dimes, and quarters,
and added the dollars, too, I'd be Gates-level wealthy.
And I'd give them all to God, the hungry, the homeless,
or just throw them to the wind
to hear her say those things just one more time.

Sue Curtis - Troy, OH

Dear Mom,

You died one week before my birthday, and we buried you the day before. My heart was aching not only for this loss but also because my birthday would always be a reminder of the emptiness of those days. This would be the first time in which I would not receive a "Happy Birthday" nor a gift nor a card from you, my first best friend.

I woke up that birthday morning in late July with a gulp in my throat and a tear in my eye. Bonnie stayed with me overnight, and we sat down to have our sisterly cup of coffee. Next to the cup was a Hallmark bag. With trembling hands, I opened it to find two cards, for which you shopped early, signed by you! Could you have known . . . ?

The verses in both cards were especially poignant but one particularly so. It reads in part, "I hope that when things get complicated or challenging, you'll remember how strong and talented you are and know that you have what it takes to handle anything that might come along."

Now, every year, I pull out those birthday cards and read them. It makes me feel close to you, and, thanks to you, Mom, I do have what it takes to handle anything that might come along.

My love always,
Chao

Carolyn Gingerelli - Minneapolis, MN

Mom,

I will always fondly remember, years ago, during a few warm days in July when you, Dad and Bob and I and our two children met at a resort. We shared a little cabin on the shore of a sandy lake. We normally didn't get to see you very often because of the miles between us, so this would prove to be a real treat. I cherished being able to talk to you at leisure. I loved us cooking together and sharing time with you and Dad. It was nice to see my small kids enjoying their grandparents.

It was so wonderful that you were in remission from cancer. One day in that little cabin, you told me, "I dreamed I died on the Fourth of July." You had a twinkle in your eye, and the look on your face showed the dream was most magnificent. As you told this, your voice was like a joyous song. While describing it, you turned your eyes upward and told me while everyone was gazing up at fireworks, the sky opened up and Jesus took you to heaven. I could tell you were awed by this amazing dream. You then, in jest, said you always knew you would go out with a bang.

The vacation came to an end, and I didn't give your dream another thought until four years later. Cancer had returned, and on the Fourth of July in the early morning hours, you died with a smile on your face. Even though there were no fireworks at that time of day that I could see, I have to wonder if you might have seen the most awesome fireworks display ever.

Thank you, Mom, for that special time together and for sharing your dream with me.

Patricia Anderson - Webster, WI

My mother and I shared a lot in common. From the fairness of our skin to our love of our Irish heritage, we were best friends as well as mother and daughter.

In 2000, my mother joined my family and me on a trip to Ireland to celebrate my 20th wedding anniversary. She almost didn't go. Something told me to make it happen! I even paid for half of her trip.

My husband and I renewed our vows in Galway Cathedral, and it was just us, our 2 children, and my mother. It was quite a momentous day.

On that trip, my mother pulled me aside in Killarney and told me that she believed it would be her last trip to Ireland. Now, considering she had been there at least a dozen times before and didn't show any the worse for wear than I was, I found this shocking! I told her that if I went back, which I fully intended to do, she was going with me! She said she just felt like she wasn't going to make it back.

I said that I was glad she went with us then. I then chalked it up to her being tired.

In September of 2001, we attended a wedding for my cousin. I spoke to her up until midnight that night. We had to catch up on what we thought about what everybody was wearing and all of the other good stuff! We said good night and "I love you," and she said she was going to bed.

My father was babysitting for my sister that night. He came home the next morning and found my mother dead in the bathroom. She never made it to bed. I was the last one to speak with her. The last words she said to me were, "I love you."

That very final lesson from my mother was, always say "I love you" when you speak to someone. You just never know when it will be the last time.

I thank my mother not only for that lesson but for that final "I love you."

Coleen McCrea Katz - Havertown, PA

I used to think that Heaven
Was forever and a day
That once a soul departed
It was oh, so far away

Out of reach for those of us
Whom it has left behind
But since you've gone to Heaven, Mom,
I've had a change of mind

'Cause I can feel your guidance
In all that I pursue
And I can feel you close to me
Each time that I need you

I haven't lost your kindness,
Your humor, nor your love
And I still feel your kisses
And your precious loving touch

Thank you, Mom, for everything
Your tender love and care
For all the fun and laughter
And the happiness we shared

And thank you for the loving way
You gently molded me
To follow in your footsteps
When your soul was finally freed

Your things are all here with me
And they're such a part of you
That every time I look at them
I'm looking at you, too

I used to think that Heaven
Was forever and a day
But knowing you're in Heaven
It's not that far away

I love you, Mom!

Connie Pullen - Eagle Creek, OR

If you have enjoyed this book
or it has touched your life in some way,
we would love to hear from you.

Please send your comments to:
Hallmark Book Feedback
P.O. Box 419034
Mail Drop 215
Kansas City, MO 64141

Or e-mail us at:
booknotes@hallmark.com